A Practical Guide to the Law in relation to Japanese Knotweed and Other Invasive Plants

Second Edition

Tom Carter is a barrister at Ropewalk Chambers. He has been consistently ranked as a leading barrister for property law, with the 2021 edition of the Legal 500 recognising that he is: "*a particularly notable figure within the team for his specialism in cases relating to Japanese knotweed, having recently appeared in several agenda-setting nuisance, misrepresentation and professional negligence cases around infestations of the invasive species*".

Tom acted as sole counsel for the successful claimant, Mr Williams, in the case of *Network Rail v Williams* [2018] EWCA Civ 1514, the leading case on liability in nuisance for Japanese knotweed.

Since writing the first edition of this book, Tom acted as sole counsel for the claimant, Mr Davies, in *Davies v Bridgend County Borough Council*, at trial all the way up to the Supreme Court. In the Court of Appeal's decision in that case, it was held that damages for diminution in value of a property due to the presence of knotweed are not irrecoverable pure economic loss [2023] EWCA Civ 80.

In the Supreme Court's decision in that case, the issue was causation. Something which was said in the judgment of Lord Burrows "has rarely been the focus of attention in cases of the tort of private nuisance" [2024] UKSC 15.

Tom also appeared in *Churchill v Merthyr Tydfil Borough Council* [2023] EWCA Civ 1416 which was a knotweed case but had a much wider reaching effect on all civil cases. In that case, the longstanding view from the famous case of *Halsey* that parties could not be compelled to mediate was held to be obiter and thus no longer applied.

A Practical Guide to the Law in relation to Japanese Knotweed and Other Invasive Plants

Second Edition

Tom Carter

Barrister, Inner Temple

Law Brief Publishing

Published 2024 by Law Brief Publishing, an imprint of Law Brief Publishing Ltd
30 The Parks
Minehead
Somerset
TA24 8BT

www.lawbriefpublishing.com

Paperback: 978-1-916698-52-9

To Minha

PREFACE

Japanese knotweed is an invasive plant, introduced to the UK in the mid-nineteenth century. It was introduced as an ornamental plant but now is estimated to affect over 2% of development sites and 1.25% of residential properties, according to a House of Commons report in 2019.

Even if your home is not affected by Japanese knotweed, there is no escape from it: if you sell your home, you will have to declare whether or not the property is affected by it when completing the Law Society's property information form. There is a specific question and preamble at question 7.8 of that TA6 form.

An entire industry has developed around treating Japanese knotweed: on any motorway, it will not be long before you see a van emblazoned with the logo of one of the many companies including the words "Japanese knotweed" in their name. No doubt the van will be on its way to carry out treatment at yet another affected property.

At the time of writing the first edition of this book, there was only one binding authority on Japanese knotweed, in the form of the Court of Appeal's decision in *Williams v Network Rail Infrastructure Ltd* [2019] QB 601, [2018] EWCA Civ 1514. This was a landmark case establishing that the mere presence of Japanese knotweed within a claimant's boundaries is enough to constitute a nuisance without the need for physical damage.

Since then, *Davies v Bridgend County Borough Council* has confirmed two things: first, per the Court of Appeal, that damages for diminution in value are not irrecoverable pure economic loss: [2023] EWCA Civ 80. Secondly, per the Supreme Court, that ordinary principles of 'but for' causation apply to nuisance claims: [2024] UKSC 15.

Further, it was previously thought that the so-called "seven-metre rule" for Japanese knotweed was exaggerated. It was previously said that knotweed rhizomes might extend up to 7m in any direction from visible knotweed stems. There were questions over the extent of damage which Japanese knotweed can cause to properties. In February 2022, the Royal Institute of Chartered Surveyors published a document called "Japanese knotweed and residential property". It was initially published as a guidance note but then upgraded to a professional standard in October 2022.

The aim of this book is to give a concise but comprehensive summary of the principles and how they will apply. This should give you a steady footing for any claim, be it in nuisance, professional negligence or misrepresentation, whether you act for a claimant or a defendant

The law quoted in this book is believed to be accurate as at 30 August 2024.

Tom Carter
August 2024

CONTENTS

PART ONE

NUISANCE CLAIMS

CHAPTER ONE

THE ELEMENTS OF A NUISANCE CLAIM

To establish a claim in nuisance, a claimant must show that the defendant owed them a duty of care, was in breach of that duty and the breach of duty caused the claimant loss.

Before getting onto those points, however, the claimant must first show that there is something which is capable of being an actionable nuisance in the first place. The aim of this chapter is to consider what needs to be satisfied for a claimant to show a nuisance from the presence of Japanese knotweed.

To establish a nuisance, a claimant must show that:

a) There is Japanese knotweed within the boundaries of their land;

b) It has encroached onto their land from the defendant's land.

Unlike claims for encroachment of tree roots, there is no need to show physical damage in order to establish a nuisance in relation to Japanese knotweed.

This was established in the leading case on liability for Japanese knotweed in the Court of Appeal's decision in *Williams v Network Rail Infrastructure Ltd* [2019] QB 601, [2018] EWCA Civ 1514.

This was a claim by two neighbours, both of whom owned houses that backed onto a railway line owned by Network Rail. There was Japanese knotweed growing on the railway embankment adjacent to their houses. At trial, the Recorder held that knotweed had encroached from Network

Rail's land onto the claimants' land but that there was no physical damage.

The Recorder considered the three types of nuisance set out by Lord Lloyd in *Hunter v Canary Wharf* [1997] AC 655 at 695C:

i. Nuisance by encroachment on a neighbour's land;

ii. Nuisance by direct physical injury to a neighbour's land;

iii. Nuisance by interference with a neighbour's quiet enjoyment of their land.

He held that on the authorities, a type 1 nuisance nevertheless required physical damage. On that basis, he held that there was no actionable type 1 nuisance.

A type 2 nuisance was never in issue because there was no evidence of physical damage.

The Recorder did find an actionable type 3 nuisance. He held that the presence of Japanese knotweed on the defendant's land, close to the boundary with the claimants' land, was sufficient to interfere with their quiet enjoyment of their land because it may nevertheless affect the sale price and this was an interference with their quiet enjoyment of the land.

In the Court of Appeal, the Master of the Rolls warned against a rigid categorisation of nuisance claims in this way (para 41) but to explain the decision, I will use the type 1 and type 3 analysis above. The Court of Appeal took the opposite approach to the Recorder and held that there was a type 1 nuisance but not a type 3 nuisance.

The Court of Appeal held that unlike tree roots, Japanese knotweed is in itself a hazard and that it will diminish the amenity value of land even without physical damage. On that basis, a claimant need only show the presence of knotweed on their land. At para 55 it was said:

> *"Its presence, and indeed the mere presence of its rhizomes, imposes an immediate burden on the owner of the land in terms of an increased difficulty in the ability to develop, and in the cost of developing, the land, should the owner wish to do so. As the RICS paper observed, any improvement or alteration of the property requiring the removal of contaminated soil would require disposal of the soil either on site or, more likely, off site by special, and probably expensive, procedures. For all those reasons, Japanese knotweed and its rhizomes can fairly be described, in the sense of the decided cases, as a "natural hazard". They affect the owner's ability fully to use and enjoy the land. They are a classic example of an interference with the amenity value of the land."*

And at para 73:

> *"In short, there is no reason why the legal position concerning nuisance caused by the encroachment of the branches or roots of trees should undermine the right of the claimants in the present case to claim damages for nuisance by reason of the encroachment of Japanese knotweed and its rhizomes from NR's land."*

It should be noted in respect of the increased difficulty in developing land referred to in para 55 that there was no evidence from either of the claimants about plans to develop the land. It is the difficulty in principle that constitutes the interference.

The Court of Appeal did, however, reject the Recorder's finding that presence of knotweed on the defendant's land close to the boundary was enough to establish a type 3 nuisance per para 46:

> *"The Recorder's conclusion that the presence of knotweed on NR's land within seven metres of the claimants' properties was an actionable nuisance simply because it diminished the market*

> *value of the claimants' respective properties, because of lender caution in such situations, was wrong in principle."*

In the first edition of this book, I said that this paragraph had caused confusion amongst some lawyers who took it as authority that a claimant cannot recover damages for diminution in value at all. I said that this was wrong and discussed this issue in Chapter Six.

What I said in the previous edition of this book was held to be right by the Court of Appeal in *Davies v Bridgend County Borough Council* [2023] EWCA 80. In that case, the defendant argued that the diminution in value was pure economic loss because there was no physical damage, and that the reference to "simply because it diminished the market value" in para 46 of *Williams* was authority that damages for diminution could not be recovered.

In *Davies*, Birss LJ said at paras 38 and 39:

> *"38. In a case in which the knotweed is on the defendant's land, even if it is close to the boundary and at risk of invading the claimant's land, Williams holds that the reduction in market value of the claimant's land which this causes does not result from physical damage nor from physical interference with the claimant's property and therefore does not amount to a nuisance. Putting a small gloss on the opening words in paragraph 48 of Williams, I would say that the purpose of the tort of nuisance is not simply to protect the value of property. After all Williams itself later recognises that if the value of the claimant's property is diminished as a result of an interference with the claimant's quiet enjoyment or amenity, due to physical encroachment of knotweed from the defendant's land into the claimant's land, damages including diminution in value of the property will be available. Putting it another way, the reasoning in paragraph 48 of Williams, which the judges below relied on, is nothing to do with recoverability of damages in a case in which the tort of nuisance is complete.*

39. Subject to one further point I would therefore allow the claimant's appeal and turn to the respondent's notice. The reasoning at the end of paragraph 19 of the Circuit Judge's judgment is flawed because once it is accepted that there was damage leading to a loss (the diminution in value) which was consequential on the nuisance, there is no authority that consequential damage to the claimant's economic interests is irrecoverable."

The case of *Davies* subsequently went to the Supreme Court [2024] UKSC 15. The defendant conceded the point about diminution in value being a consequential loss and thus recoverable. Instead, the sole point on that appeal was causation which I will discuss later in Chapter Five.

CHAPTER TWO

ENCROACHMENT

Once a claimant establishes that there is Japanese knotweed within the boundaries of their land, it is then necessary to show that it encroached onto that land from the defendant's land. If not, the presence of Japanese knotweed may be a nuisance but it was not caused by the Defendant. On that basis, the claim fails for causation.

In some cases, encroachment may be easy to prove. For instance, if there is a large stand of mature knotweed on the defendant's land and a small amount of knotweed on the claimant's land then this would suggest that it must have spread from the larger growth on the defendant's land.

This is not always the case and it can be dangerous to make assumptions. There may be other reasons for differences in size or maturity of knotweed such as different subsoil, the presence of hard-standings obstructing growth or the effects of herbicide treatment.

The question of encroachment will nearly always turn on expert evidence from a Japanese knotweed expert. There is no technical name for these experts: they may be horticulturalists but they are not normally referred to as such in the context of knotweed claims, unlike arboriculturists in tree root claims. They are simply referred to as "Japanese knotweed experts".

Any reputable knotweed expert will be registered with the Property Care Association (PCA).

There are often initial reports which may be written with one eye on potential litigation but which are not usually CPR part 35 compliant. Claimants will often contact a treatment company before contacting solicitors so the initial report may well be the earliest detailed record of the state of the knotweed. There will usually be a plan showing the locations of knotweed and photographs. For that reason, the reports are often referred back to at trial as lay evidence but they may not go into detailed considerations of encroachment.

Ultimately the question is a simple one in most cases: is it more likely than not that the Japanese knotweed on the claimant's land originated from the defendant's land?

There may be Japanese knotweed on more than one adjacent property. This may complicate a claim if the ages and sizes of the various stands of Japanese knotweed are similar. Generally, this will be something that the Japanese knotweed expert needs to consider.

Sometimes, knotweed on adjacent properties may be a red herring if the knotweed is not right up to the boundary. For instance, if two adjacent properties back onto a strip of land with Japanese knotweed but the knotweed on each property is spread quite far apart, this might suggest that they are simply two separate stands of knotweed.

Sometimes, it may be established that Japanese knotweed has encroached onto a claimant's land from multiple properties. If so, this may raise a question about concurrent causes which I consider in the context of causation in Chapter Five.

An important question will also be *when* Japanese knotweed encroached. Not only is this often crucial in misrepresentation claims but in nuisance claims as well.

That is because if Japanese knotweed encroached before a defendant came under a duty to treat it, the defendants can argue that the claim fails the but for test. The Supreme Court confirmed in *Davies v Bridgend County Borough Council* [2024] UKSC 15 that the 'but for test' applies to nuisance claims.

What is left open, however, is a question of whether a defendant's continued failure to treat has prolonged the claimant's diminution in value. It is common for expert surveyors to say there is a tapering off period once knotweed has been treated. If treatment is successful and it does not reemerge, a reasonable buyer in the market will become less concerned about historic knotweed over time. In *Davies*, there was no evidence about this but this is now inevitably a part of the evidence in any knotweed claim.

For example, if the defendant is found to have had actual or constructive knowledge from 2012 but then did not treat until 2020, the claimant may argue that even if knotweed had already encroached before the defendant's date of knowledge, the defendant's ongoing failure to treat prevented the claimant from treating their own land because it would be futile to treat if knotweed would just re-encroach.

This is likely to be one of the key battlegrounds in nuisance claims involving knotweed following *Davies*.

CHAPTER THREE

DUTY OF CARE

Once it is shown that there is Japanese knotweed within the boundaries of a claimant's land and that it is more likely than not that it has spread from the defendant's land, in what circumstances does the defendant owe a duty of care?

The starting point is that it is immaterial whether or not the defendant planted the knotweed or actively caused it to grow or spread. It is well-established that a defendant may be liable for a nuisance if they adopt or continue it: *Sedleigh Denfield v O'Callaghan* [1940] AC 880 (HL). In this context, to continue a nuisance means to fail to take reasonable steps to prevent it i.e. non-feasance. This rule extends to liability for naturals hazards and not only man-made ones: *Leakey v National Trust* [1980] QB 485 (CA).

Therefore, the question is when the defendant did or should have known both of the following: first, knowledge that Japanese knotweed is an invasive plant and secondly, that Japanese knotweed was present on the defendant's land.

Depending on the type of defendant, the first or second of these may be the key issue. For instance, a local authority with thousands of acres of land may have known for some time that Japanese knotweed is an invasive plant but may argue that it did not know that there was Japanese knotweed in an area of one of its parks.

Conversely, a residential homeowner with a small garden would be bound to know that Japanese knotweed was present if it was there to be seen from the kitchen window but might argue that they did not know that it was an invasive plant.

In terms of knowledge, this can be actual knowledge or constructive knowledge. Within the ambit of constructive knowledge, there is also the question of specialist knowledge.

Actual knowledge is straightforward: it is when the defendant actually knew of the knotweed. The key evidence is usually a record of any complaints from the claimant or someone nearby. Sometimes, a local resident will complain about Japanese knotweed to the council and an environmental officer will visit or send a letter to the defendant. Sometimes, actual knowledge might be inferred from the fact that the defendant was seen trying to remove the knotweed by a neighbour.

Arguments on actual knowledge will usually come down to the strength of the evidence. Defendants will often deny having received a complaint unless there is a written record of it. Where there is a letter from the council, it will nearly always be denied that this was received.

Against institutional defendants such as Network Rail, the Environment Agency or local authorities, not only may there be evidence of former complaints about Japanese knotweed from other properties but there will usually be other documents showing treatment records or policies for treating Japanese knotweed. All of this will show actual knowledge about Japanese knotweed being an invasive plant. The battleground will then be knowledge of knotweed in a particular location.

Constructive knowledge is based on what a reasonable person in the defendant's position should have known: the defendant is then fixed with that knowledge.

In *Williams v Network Rail Infrastructure Ltd* [2019] QB 601, [2018] EWCA Civ 1514, there was no challenge in the Court of Appeal to the Recorder's finding at trial that Network Rail had constructive knowledge that Japanese knotweed was an invasive plant and that it was present near to the claimants' homes from 2012/13.

Given that finding was made in the County Court, it is not binding, but all other judges have followed this approach in Japanese knotweed claims. For instance in *Davies v Bridgend County Borough Council* [2024] UKSC 15, the judge's finding at trial was that the defendant had constructive knowledge from 2012/13 and was in breach from 2013 until it started to treat in 2018.

The reasoning for that approach is that from 2012 onwards, there was a marked shift in terms of awareness of the dangers of Japanese knotweed. Its invasiveness had been known about for some time before this but in 2012, there was guidance published from RICS ("Japanese knotweed and residential property") about the dangers of Japanese knotweed. It was held that following this, a reasonable person in the defendant's position should have known about it.

The reasoning for the 2012/13 rather than simply 2012 was to allow some time thereafter to identify knotweed near to the claimants' properties in the course of carrying out a reasonable system of inspection.

Where the defendant owns large amounts of land, arguments on inspection will often be key. Defendants will argue that it would be an unduly onerous burden to expect regular inspections of large amounts of land and may seek to rely on a purely reactive system based on complaints. Claimants will argue that this a system of proactive inspection is reasonably required given the dangers of Japanese knotweed and that staff should also be trained to identify it while on the defendant's land doing other work.

There is no binding authority on what is required in terms of inspection. The decision in *Williams* suggests that a year was a reasonable period though there may be different factors at play for different defendants.

I should note that in one case, I have seen reference to an unreported decision of the County Court of *Flanagan v Wigan Metropolitan Borough Council* said to be from 1995. The only source of this case that can be found is reference to it in an online blog and reference to it in evidence given by a knotweed treatment provider to the Parliamentary Committee which was considering Japanese knotweed and whose report led to the recommendation for the updated 2022 RICS paper.

The description of that case is that in 1995, a homeowner obtained an injunction against Wigan Council to compel them to treat a 1 metre strip of knotweed along the boundary with the claimant's land for three years and to install a reinforced concrete boundary wall to prevent further spread.

It remains to be seen whether this mysterious case will ever in fact be unearthed. Against a particular defendant, it may raise a question of specialist knowledge.

What then of specialist knowledge? This is a concept flowing from the Supreme Court's decision in the case of *Baker v Quantum Clothing Group Ltd* [2011] UKSC 17. A defendant with subjectively higher knowledge will be held to a higher standard than another defendant without that knowledge.

This approach has been expressly adopted into nuisance cases involving tree roots in *Khan v Harrow Council & Kane* [2013] EWHC 2687 (TCC). There, the subjective approach was described as creating a floor not a ceiling.

The effect of this is that all defendants are held to the same objective standard, and no defendant can rely on its own subjective ignorance to lower that standard, but a defendant who does have specialist knowledge on a subject will be held to that higher standard.

In the context of a Japanese knotweed claim, this may mean that a professional gardener would be held to a higher standard when considering constructive knowledge than a layperson.

For large institutional defendants, disclosure of policies, documents and records relating to Japanese knotweed will be important because it may transpire that a particular defendant did have specialist knowledge.

There is some overlap with actual knowledge. For instance, a defendant may be found to have known about the invasiveness of Japanese knotweed from at least the 2000s. On that point, the defendant had actual knowledge of this fact. The claimant would then argue that based on this, the defendant should have implemented a system of inspection in the 2000s and therefore had constructive knowledge of Japanese knotweed near to the claimant's property within one year of that date because it would or should have been discovered on a reasonable inspection.

CHAPTER FOUR

BREACH OF DUTY

Once a defendant has knowledge of Japanese knotweed, in principle and in a particular location, it comes under a duty to do something about it. What is required of a defendant in order to comply with its duty?

As in any case, the standard required in order to comply with the duty is not one of perfection. It is an objective question of reasonableness, having regard to all the circumstances of the case. This principle can be found in a multitude of authorities in all areas of the common law but in this context, the case of *Vernon Knight Associates v Cornwall Council* [2013] EWCA Civ 950 is relevant.

The three key points from that decision are as follows:

i. The defendant owes a "measured duty" to take reasonable care to prevent damage to a neighbouring claimant from natural hazards on its land.

ii. The court will consider what is fair, just and reasonable, taking into account the extent of foreseeable risk, the availability of preventative measures and their cost and the resources of both parties.

iii. Where the defendant is a public authority with substantial resources, the court will consider the competing demands on those resources.

The duty is often referred to as a duty to treat. This is convenient shorthand because that will normally be the minimum standard expected of any defendant. Despite the problems caused by Japanese knotweed, the process to get rid of it is fairly straightforward (albeit it still takes a long period of time).

The knotweed can be treated with herbicide or it can be excavated. I will discuss damages for treatment costs in Chapter Seven, but herbicide treatment is generally cheaper because it does not involve excavating potentially huge quantities of soil. There are plenty of reputable treatment companies who will implement a four to five-year herbicide treatment plan with insurance-backed guarantee for a modest sum, usually between £3,000 to £5,000.

Given this, even if the defendant is an individual with limited means, or argues that as a public authority it has other competing demands on its resources, it is difficult to see how it would escape a finding that it was required to implement a system of herbicide treatment in order to comply with its duty. Certainly, that was the finding of the Recorder at trial in *Williams v Network Rail Infrastructure Ltd* [2019] QB 601, [2018] EWCA Civ 1514, not then challenged on appeal.

Depending on the defendant, it may use its own staff to treat the knotweed or may engage a third-party contractor. The benefit to the defendant of using its own staff may be cost but those advising a defendant should be aware of the risks involved in this approach. I have seen many cases, acting for both claimants and defendants, of employees purporting to carry out herbicide treatment which has not been done properly.

For instance, the knotweed must be sprayed methodically and consistently. Japanese knotweed experts will often be able to identify signs of herbicide treatment from "bonsai growth", which is generally weakened growth with signs of stem twisting. This is characteristic of the rhizomes from which those stems have grown being treated with herbicide.

Where the stand of knotweed is large, it is often the case that parts will be missed. If so, some stems will show signs of herbicide treatment but others will not. The knotweed which has not been treated will then continue to grow unabated.

Arguments on the quality of herbicide treatment do not go to a resources argument. Once a defendant begins to treat, it costs no more to do this properly than to do it badly.

There are other factors which may undermine the effectiveness of herbicide treatment: for example, spraying on a very windy day or attending the site shortly after herbicide treatment and cutting down the stems before the herbicide has had time to translocate to the rhizomes.

Where treatment has taken place, it will be important for a defendant to keep a proper record of treatment. At a minimum, this should normally involve recording the weather conditions, the herbicide used and the dosage rate together with the metres squared of knotweed which has been sprayed. If a defendant does not keep these records, it may run into difficulties later in proving that treatment has been reasonable.

There are often also difficulties with plans showing a stand of knotweed growing in an area behind a row of houses. It can sometimes be difficult to ascertain if and when knotweed was treated behind a particular claimant's house. Any defendant will be well advised to keep detailed records of precisely what has been treated, not simply general references to areas.

It will also be important to have a treatment plan in place and for herbicide to be sprayed consistently. Normally, a treatment plan will involve the application of herbicide once or twice per year. If a defendant begins treatment but then misses a year, that missed year may well amount to a breach of duty.

If a defendant uses its own employees to treat the knotweed, it will also be important to be able to evidence the training and qualifications of those staff.

In order to consider the reasonableness of treatment, it will normally be required for parties to rely on expert evidence from a Japanese knotweed expert. This will usually be the same expert who has commented on encroachment as discussed in Chapter Two.

There are certain circumstances where it may be inferred that treatment has not been done reasonably. For instance, if a defendant has purported to treat a stand of knotweed for over five years but there is little, if any, sign of the stand reducing in size, the court may infer that it has not been done properly.

Effective herbicide treatment will reduce the size of a stand of knotweed on a proportional basis meaning that the same rate of reduction should be expected in a large stand as in a small stand. While there is no hard and fast rule, certainly it would normally be expected that the knotweed has been eradicated or almost eradicated after four or five years.

The court will inevitably allow some leeway but if there has been little significant reduction in the knotweed after five years, this does tend to suggest that it has not been treated properly.

CHAPTER FIVE

CAUSATION

Any nuisance claim must follow the basic proposition that in order to recover damages, a claimant must prove that those damages have been caused by the defendant's breach of duty.

The first question is the date of encroachment of Japanese knotweed. Where knotweed encroached before the defendant came under a duty to treat it, the Supreme Court's decision in *Davies v Bridgend County Borough Council* [2024] UKSC 15 is now authority that the 'but for' test applies to nuisance claims.

The effect of this is that a claimant will not be able to recover for treatment or general damages since those losses were always incurred but for any breach. In *Davies*, the same approach was taken to diminution in value, but there was no evidence on the question of any tapering off of the diminution over time. That is now likely to be a more central feature of all nuisance claims with historic encroachment. In principle, it is compatible with the 'but for' test to assert that if the defendant had treated from 2013, the knotweed would have been successfully treated by 2017 and the claimant could likewise have treated their own land. If in fact the defendant did not start treating until 2020, that delay of seven years would mean that the tapering off would be delayed by seven years and so the claimant would seek the additional cost of that.

There are all sorts of other potential issues on causation. For example, what if Japanese knotweed on the claimant's land is found to have spread from two neighbouring properties, each owned by a separate defendant? What if only one of those defendants is found to have been in breach of duty: would the defendant in breach be liable for the whole loss, a portion of the loss or none of the loss?

The courts have grappled with similar issues in other areas. One relevant question may be whether losses caused by Japanese knotweed are divisible or indivisible. Divisible losses are dose-related (for example, damage to hearing caused by noise). The need for treatment and diminution in value will tend to arise as long as there is *any* knotweed present at a property. On that basis, it would seem to be an indivisible loss.

There is authority, in the context of defamation, that defendants are liable for the whole of an indivisible loss: *Dingle v Associated Newspapers* [1972] AC 601 (HL). There, the House of Lords held that a claimant's damages following a defamatory newspaper article did not fall to be reduced because his reputation had already been harmed by things said about him in Parliament, where a cause of action was barred by privilege.

While it is a separate cause of action to nuisance, defamation is still founded in tort (albeit now supplemented by statute in the Defamation Act 2013). The authorities are clear that there is no real difference between negligence and nuisance, instead those simply being labels to deal with the question of a reasonable apportionment of responsible conduct between neighbours: *Delaware Mansions v Lord Mayor* [2001] UKHL 55. The court might conclude that in this context, the same approach to causation as in *Dingle* should apply in nuisance.

CHAPTER SIX

DIMINUTION IN VALUE

A claim for diminution in value is often the most hotly contested issue in a nuisance case. The simple reason for this is that it is usually the largest head of loss, normally by a significant margin.

Before considering the legal concepts, the starting point is that there will always need to be expert valuation evidence from a surveyor to deal with diminution in value. The surveyor's job is ultimately to value the property without Japanese knotweed and then to compare this to its value with Japanese knotweed. The difference is the diminution in value.

Sometimes, an expert surveyor will not have knowledge of the local property market in the area of the claimant's property and so it is often the case that they will be assisted by valuations from local estate agents. The surveyor can normally be asked if they would prefer this before they are formally instructed: if so, valuations from local estate agents can be obtained and then sent to the surveyor with their instructions.

There are two kinds of diminution in value. These tend to be referred to as full diminution in value and residual diminution in value.

Full diminution in value is the difference in price between the property without knotweed and with knotweed that remains untreated.

Residual diminution in value is the difference in price between the property without knotweed and with Japanese knotweed but after a treatment plan with an insurance-backed guarantee is in place.

The figure for full diminution in value will be higher, but in all cases the court is overwhelmingly likely to award the lower figure for the residual diminution in value plus treatment costs.

The reason for this is that damages for full diminution in value would tend to over-compensate a claimant. Take an example of a property worth £200,000. An expert surveyor values it at £150,000 with Japanese knotweed. The full diminution figure is £50,000. With a treatment plan in place costing £4,000, the property would be worth £180,000. The residual diminution is £20,000 and treatment would cost £4,000 (so damages are £24,000 in total).

In those circumstances, were the court to award damages for full diminution of £50,000 then the claimant could spend £4,000 on treatment, have that diminution reduced to £20,000 and then have a windfall of £26,000 (£50,000 minus £24,000).

It is therefore crucial to ensure that the surveyor is instructed to comment on the value of the property without knotweed and the residual diminution in value. They may also comment on the full diminution but that figure is unlikely to be relevant.

There are two main causes of diminution in value. The first is lender caution. It has been the case before that many mortgage lenders simply would not lend a purchaser money to buy a house where Japanese knotweed was present. Often this would be detected during the mortgage valuation report. Sometimes, an owner would only discover the presence of Japanese knotweed when trying to re-mortgage and a surveyor would then identify it. The consequence of lender caution is that if trying to sell their home, a claimant might only be able to sell to cash buyers or at auction, usually for less money.

The issue of lender caution has become less of a problem in recent years because most (or at least many) mortgage lenders will now lend against properties as long as there is a treatment plan with insurance-backed guarantee in place.

The second and main cause of diminution in value is purchaser stigma. Often, a buyer might make an offer on a home which is accepted but they later obtain a survey which identifies Japanese knotweed. Alternatively, the seller may declare that the property is affected by Japanese knotweed at question 7.8 of the Law Society's property information form (considered in Chapter Eleven) as they are bound to do if they know that it is present.

If so, the buyer may well pull out or insist on a lower price. Though Japanese knotweed can be treated effectively, the process takes many years and it may later re-emerge. In the meantime, the use of that area of the property will be restricted and if the buyers later wanted to sell the property, they themselves would have to declare that it was affected by Japanese knotweed.

The consequence of this is that for many purchasers, they may simply decide that it is too uncertain and too much hassle, and would rather buy a similar property nearby that does not have knotweed.

In terms of figures, generally one would see a residual diminution in value in the region of 3-5% for a residential property. This will of course depend on the surveyor's evidence in a particular case and there may well be factors to justify a higher or lower percentage than this.

For commercial properties, the same principles of diminution in value apply. The surveyor will need to take the nature of the property into consideration when assessing diminution in value but ultimately the approach is similar.

Since the updated RICS guidance was published in 2022, my experience of expert evidence from surveyors is that this has not had an impact. The reason for this is that the same principles of purchaser caution still apply: someone may simply not want the hassle of worrying about Japanese knotweed if they can buy a similar property without it.

The reality is that most purchasers will be uninformed and would simply prefer to err on the side of caution and not take the risk. It is no consolation to a property owner who can only sell their property at a reduced value to say that the purchasers refusing to buy it for more are being irrational.

In those circumstances, I would suggest that the question is who should bear the burden of that risk. It seems to me that the only sensible answer to this is that the tortfeasor must bear the risk: that is consistent with the law's approach in other areas.

CHAPTER SEVEN

TREATMENT COSTS

The normal approach for the court to take when assessing damages for nuisance from Japanese knotweed is to look at the residual diminution in value of the property plus the cost of treatment.

I discuss diminution in value in Chapter Six: the residual diminution is the diminution in value once a treatment plan and insurance-backed guarantee is in place.

If the court does award damages for the residual diminution, the claimant should be entitled to the costs of treatment because it is only that treatment which enables a claimant to mitigate their loss and to reduce the diminution in value from the full figure to the residual figure.

First, should treatment costs be for herbicide treatment or for excavation?

Herbicide treatment is usually the cheaper option and involves a four to five-year treatment plan where Japanese knotweed will be sprayed with a herbicide (usually glyphosate) once or twice per year until eradicated. The herbicide can either be applied with a sprayer or injected into the knotweed stems. This is done during the growing season and the herbicide translocates into the rhizomes, stopping the plant from growing.

The knotweed is considered to be successfully treated when there is no more visual growth during a growing season. There will likely still be rhizomes in the soil which may remain dormant for up to 20 years so it is not truly eradicated. At this point, there should be a 10-year insurance-backed guarantee that then begins. This is a guarantee that if knotweed re-emerges within that 10-year period from eradication, the treatment provider will re-attend and start a new course of treatment.

The insurance provides reassurance to the property owner that if the treatment provider ceases trading during that time, the policy will fund the cost of another provider.

Excavation involves removing all soil potentially contaminated by Japanese knotweed rhizomes. There are various methods of doing this employed by different treatment companies but the most straightforward is often referred to as "dig and dump". It involves, as the name suggests, simply digging out the soil and disposing of it.

Excavation is usually more expensive, not least because it will tend to involve excavating very large amounts of soil. Rhizomes can be present quite deep into the ground and are known to have a lateral spread.

Excavation should also be followed with an insurance-backed guarantee to cover the possibility that some knotweed has been missed.

Claimants will often prefer excavation because it is a quicker solution than herbicide treatment. Inevitably, defendants will be unlikely to want to pay the additional costs of excavation when herbicide treatment, if done properly, is known to be effective.

There are also downsides to excavation in certain circumstances: for instance, if rhizomes are present in concrete foundations, they cannot be excavated without undermining the structure. Herbicide treatment can, however, be applied to knotweed stems growing from those rhizomes and it will then translocate into the rhizomes beneath the structure.

There is an argument that while the costs of excavation are greater, it may reduce the residual diminution in value of the property. I discuss this in the context of diminution in Chapter Six but in conclusion, I think it is unlikely that this is really the case. Given the cheaper cost of herbicide treatment, this is another indicator that in most cases, the court will tend towards herbicide costs rather than excavation.

There are some exceptions to this. For instance, the claimant may be a building developer with a limited period of time to finish building homes before planning permission expires. In certain circumstances, the additional costs of excavation may be justified.

In either case, there will need to be a quote for treatment costs. Often, an early quote is obtained by the claimant pre-litigation. The parties will generally be wise to obtain up-to-date quotes at the time of any updated schedule of loss and counter-schedule.

The other question is the presence of a root barrier. Whether there is herbicide treatment or excavation, the purpose of a root barrier is to stop knotweed from re-encroaching from the defendant's land. Whether the court awards this is something which will depend on the court's assessment of whether the defendant has (belatedly or not) started treating effectively and whether it is likely to do so in future.

CHAPTER EIGHT

REPAIRS AND OTHER LOSSES

While it is now thought that the danger of physical damage to houses from Japanese knotweed has been overstated, it does remain the case that it can and will cause damage to all sorts of property, including patios, garden fences and sheds.

Where there is damage, a claimant can recover for this but the crucial issue is often whether they can show that the damage was caused by the knotweed.

In certain cases, this may be straightforward. For example, damage to a patio where there are Japanese knotweed rhizomes underneath can usually be taken to have been caused by the knotweed.

In other cases, it may be difficult to establish whether damage was caused by knotweed or whether it is simply deterioration through age. For instance, a wooden boundary fence may have been in situ for decades. There may be visible damage on the part of the boundary where Japanese knotweed has encroached, suggesting that damage has been caused by the knotweed, but the fence is unlikely to be in perfect condition in other areas.

In cases where property damage from knotweed is alleged, a claimant will nearly always need expert evidence on causation. It will usually be the expert surveyor who is asked to comment on this alongside reporting on diminution in value. A defendant can likewise ask its surveyor to comment on this when providing their report.

Sometimes, certain items of garden furniture will have to be removed in order to treat Japanese knotweed at the property. For example, it is often the case that a claimant will be asked to remove a garden shed. If so, the claimant may be able to recover damages for this. Causation is usually more straightforward in this case because its removal clearly flows from the presence of Japanese knotweed. If its removal is recommended by a reputable treatment provider, it would be difficult to criticise a claimant for following this advice.

For all of these claims, the basic principle will apply that damages are valued on a like-for-like basis. In the example of a garden shed, damages would be for the value of the shed in its present condition and age, which may well be significantly less than the value of a new shed.

There are various ways in which the parties can approach this. Given the sums in dispute will generally be modest, the court may well accept an approach of looking at an invoice for the original item if available, or a quote for a new equivalent and then applying a percentage discount to account for age and pre-existing damage. If so, the percentage would normally be based on the expected lifespan of the item. A shed might be expected to last 20 years: if so, a 10-year old shed which has to be removed to allow treatment of knotweed would logically be worth 50% of a new equivalent.

Limitation will often be critical in claims for repairs and other losses. I discuss limitation for all types of claims in Chapter Twenty, and for nuisance claims in general there is the principle of a continuing nuisance. This does still provide, however, that damages incurred more than six years before the claim is brought will not be recoverable.

Claims for physical damage to fences, patios and sheds etc. will operate in the same way as physical damage in the case of subsidence from tree roots, where it is well-established that damage shown to have occurred more than six years before the claim is brought will not be recoverable.

On that basis, as well as establishing causation of damage, it will also be important to establish when damage was caused.

A claimant may also have a claim for general damages for distress and inconvenience. This is in line with similar damages in claims for subsidence from tree roots. In those cases, such damages have been described as “modest”.

In *Williams v Network Rail Infrastructure Ltd* [2019] QB 601, [2018] EWCA Civ 1514, the Recorder awarded £350 per year at trial, which was not then challenged on appeal.

In that case, there were two claimants, each the sole owner of their respective properties. Where there are co-owners, they may both be entitled to an award of general damages.

The yearly figure will depend on the extent of the Japanese knotweed and how disruptive it is. For instance, knotweed growing right up against the windows of a house will be more disruptive than a small stand of knotweed at the far end of the garden.

Ordinarily, a claimant could expect to recover an award of general damages for each year from breach of duty either to the end of the breach (if the defendant has started complying with its duty before trial) or else to date of trial.

If an owner does not live at the property, they will not be able to recover general damages during that period.

CHAPTER NINE

MITIGATION AND CONTRIBUTORY NEGLIGENCE

A common argument in nuisance claims is that the claimant has themselves been negligent or failed to mitigate their loss. This can be either by not or by not reporting it sooner, failing to treat Japanese knotweed on their own land or potentially making the situation worse by purporting to treat it but doing so poorly.

As far as a claimant reporting Japanese knotweed is concerned, any evidence of reporting is relevant to the date of the defendant's actual knowledge as discussed in Chapter Three but often this will come after the date of constructive knowledge in any event.

If so then it would be surprising for the court to make any reduction in damages to reflect contributory negligence or a failure to mitigate. The reason for this is that the defendant is already fixed with knowledge that it should reasonably have acquired. In those circumstances, it cannot rely on a claimant's failure to report because that failure made no difference: the defendant is already taken as having that knowledge in any event.

There may be circumstances, however, where a failure to report is relevant. For instance, it may be relevant where the defendant is an individual with no particular knowledge of Japanese knotweed. If a claimant were to identify Japanese knotweed on the neighbouring defendant's land but not mention it, it would be open to the court to make a finding of contributory negligence against them if the knotweed later spread.

In respect of a claimant not treating knotweed on their own land once they know it is present, this is a logical argument, but my own view is that it will rarely succeed. The reason for this is that unless and until the defendant puts in place a reasonable treatment plan for its own land, it is futile for the claimant to treat knotweed on their land because even if it is eradicated, knotweed is likely to re-encroach from the defendant's land in the future.

For these reasons, a failure to mitigate argument based on the claimant not treating knotweed on their land will not usually succeed.

There is then the argument where a claimant has actively tried to treat or remove the knotweed but has not done so in a proper way. Sometimes, laypeople will do all sorts of unwise things to try to remove knotweed. Often this will involve pulling shoots out of the ground or cutting it down. Both of these are unhelpful because they prevent the knotweed from being properly treated. The knotweed stems need to remain intact so that when herbicide is sprayed or injected, it can translocate down into the rhizomes and kill the plant. If the stems are removed or cut back, there is nowhere for the herbicide to travel.

Occasionally, a claimant will do something truly novel such as pouring petrol on the Japanese knotweed. I have seen one case where this occurred on a large stand of knotweed covering almost their entire back garden. Thankfully they did not then set it on fire.

There may be other cases where specific arguments on mitigation or contributory negligence arise. An obvious example of contributory negligence may be someone who knows there is knotweed in their back garden but then has building work done and allows the rhizomes to spread, making their situation worse.

PART TWO

ARTICLE 1
PROTOCOL 1

CHAPTER TEN

ARTICLE 1 PROTOCOL 1 CLAIMS

There are contexts where a claimant cannot rely on the tort of nuisance or some other tort to establish liability against a defendant.

For instance, where knotweed is close to his property but he cannot show encroachment. On the authority of *Williams v Network Rail Infrastructure Ltd* [2019] QB 601, [2018] EWCA Civ 1514, there cannot be a nuisance in those circumstances. There might still be liability, however, under Article 1 Protocol 1 of the ECHR ("A1P1").

Alternatively, imagine a scenario where a building developer purchases land and applies for planning permission to build a number of houses. During the planning process, local residents complain that the land is affected by Japanese knotweed. The council grants planning permission but with a condition that he treats the knotweed before commencing work. The council then delays in signing off the treatment and he cannot start the work. Either the planning permission lapses or he simply loses money while the land sits unused.

It would be difficult for a claimant to establish a cause of action in negligence against the council in those circumstances. He would struggle to establish any kind of assumption of responsibility that could give rise to a duty for pure economic loss.

In those circumstances, he might, however, have a remedy under A1P1.

Whereas a nuisance consists of an interference with the quiet use and enjoyment of land, A1P1 contains the concept of "peaceful enjoyment". The Article provides:

> *"(1) Every natural or legal person is entitled to the peaceful enjoyment of his possessions. No one shall be deprived of his possession except in the public interest and subject to the conditions provided for by law and the general principles of international law.*
>
> *(2) The preceding provisions shall not, however, in any way impair the right of a state to enforce such laws as it deems necessary to control the use of property in accordance with the general interest or to secure the payment of taxes or other contributions or penalties."*

In *Williams*, it was held that diminution in value arising from knotweed on the defendant's land, close to a claimant's land, will not amount to a nuisance. The knotweed must actually have encroached onto the claimant's land, at which point diminution in value may be a consequential loss. The reasoning for this is at para 48:

> *"The purpose of the tort of nuisance is not to protect the value of property as an investment or a financial asset."*

An A1P1 claim, by contrast, does include an economic element. The authorities relating to what amounts as a possession include shares, patents, ownership of a debt and the right to enforce a court order or decision on arbitration. These are all clearly economic interests.

In *Thomas & ors v Bridgend County Borough Council* [2011] EWCA Civ 862, the claimants sought damages for diminution in value of their homes due to noise and nuisance from a new relief road.

In that case, it was explicitly said at para 38:

> *"To summarise, loss of a quiet and pleasant environment, without evidence of loss of value, is not enough to engage Article 1"*

There are two readings of this approach:

i. A claimant needs to show loss of a quiet and pleasant enjoyment <u>and</u> a loss of value;

ii. The only relevant question is loss of value and loss of a quiet and pleasant enjoyment is irrelevant.

The remainder of the decision and the commentary referred to therein tends to suggest that the second reading is correct. That is to say, the scope of A1P1 is only concerned with economic value and a claimant need not prove both.

This suggests that a claimant who cannot show encroachment but who is affected by knotweed on a defendant's land nearby might nevertheless succeed in an A1P1 claim.

The limitation on a claim under Art 1 Protocol 1 is that it is only available against public authorities.

ECHR rights do not have direct effect but are enforceable by virtue of their inclusion in Schedule 1 to the Human Rights Act 1998. Section 6(1) of that Act provides that it is unlawful for a public authority to act in a way which is incompatible with a Convention right.

Under section 6(3) of the Act, a public authority includes "any person certain of whose functions are functions of a public nature" but under section 6(5), not if the act in question is private.

In *Cameron v Network Rail Infrastructure Ltd* [2006] EWHC 1133 (QB), it was held that Network Rail was not acting as a public authority as infrastructure controller of the national railway network at the time of the Potters Bar train crash.

Given this restrictive approach, it seems likely that an A1P1 knotweed claim against Network Rail would fail on the basis that Network Rail was not acting as a public authority.

A public authority will, of course, include councils, as can be seen from the *Thomas* case.

PART THREE

MISREPRESENTATION CLAIMS

CHAPTER ELEVEN

THE TA6 FORM

In most misrepresentation claims, the representation will come from the Law Society's property information form aka "the TA6 form".

On 8 June 2020, the Law Society published the new fourth edition of the TA6 form. For sellers completing the form after this date, they will likely have used the new form. Before this date, sellers likely used the third edition.

For both versions, the relevant section is found at question 7.8.

Both versions ask whether the property is affected by Japanese knotweed. In both, the seller can tick "Yes", "No" or "Not known".

If the seller does tick "Yes", there is a further question in both versions asking for details of any treatment plan.

The difference between the two versions is the preamble.

In the third edition, this reads:

> ***"Japanese knotweed***
>
> ***Note:*** *Japanese knotweed is an invasive plant that can cause damage to property. It can take several years to eradicate."*

The fourth addition has a more detailed preamble which reads:

*"**Japanese knotweed***

Note: *Japanese knotweed is an invasive non-native plant that can cause damage to property if left untreated. The plant consists of visible above ground growth and an invisible rhizome (root) below ground in the soil. It can take several years to control and manage through a management and treatment plan and rhizomes may remain alive below the soil even after treatment."*

Alongside the fourth edition of the TA6 form, the Law Society published updated explanatory notes in 2020. These can be found on the Law Society website at:

https://www.lawsociety.org.uk/topics/property/transaction-forms

There is no decided authority on the status of the explanatory notes in the context of knotweed but my own view is that they add little. They simply reinforce the obvious distinction between a seller answering "No" and "Not known". They then go on to explain herbicide treatment and excavation.

As well as question 7.8, the questions at 2.1 and 2.2 of the TA6 form may also be relevant.

These read:

*"**2. Disputes and complaints***

2.1 Have there been any disputes or complaints regarding this property or a property nearby? If Yes, please give details:

2.2 Is the seller aware of anything which might lead to a dispute about the property or a property nearby? If Yes, please give details:"

The seller can either tick "Yes" or "No" to these.

One can see how these questions might be relevant. For example, a seller knows that there is Japanese knotweed growing in the garden next door. They don't know whether it has actually spread onto their land and so they correctly answer "Not known" at question 7.8 of the TA6 form. They do, however, appreciate that knotweed is an invasive plant which is likely to spread at some point in the future. If they were to tick "No" to question 2.2, they may well fall foul of the word "might" in that question.

CHAPTER TWELVE

LIABILITY

In most cases the representation will come from the Law Society's property information form ("the TA6 form") as discussed above in Chapter Eleven.

Ordinarily, the best and most straightforward claim for any buyer is a claim under section 2(1) of the Misrepresentation Act 1967 ("the 1967 Act").

This provides:

> *"Where a person has entered into a contract after a misrepresentation has been made to him by another party thereto and as a result thereof he has suffered loss, then, if the person making the misrepresentation would be liable to damages in respect thereof had the misrepresentation been made fraudulently, that person shall be so liable notwithstanding that the misrepresentation was not made fraudulently, unless he proves that he had reasonable ground to believe and did believe up to the time the contract was made the facts represented were true."*

The first stage is to establish a misrepresentation.

In this respect, there are two kinds of cases, depending on whether the seller ticked "No" or "Not known" at question 7.8 of the TA6 form.

If the seller ticked "No", a claimant need only show that the property was affected by Japanese knotweed in order to show that this representation was untrue. At this stage, the seller's knowledge is irrelevant. Under section 2(1), the burden then shifts to the seller to prove that he did believe it to be true and that he had reasonable grounds to believe it.

The reasonable grounds point is crucial because it renders the question of whether the seller did actually believe it large irrelevant. Instead, in a "No" case, the crucial issue is what steps the seller took to satisfy themselves of the answer.

If the seller ticked "Not known", the buyer needs to show that the seller did know about the knotweed for there to be a misrepresentation in the first place. Of course, if this is proved, the seller could never prove that he believed it and had reasonable grounds to believe it. Therefore, in a "Not known" case, the question of the seller's knowledge becomes crucial.

For both types of claims, a claimant must show that the property was affected by knotweed. Generally, this can be shown in two ways. The first is through direct contemporaneous evidence such as surveyor's photographs, photographs from the estate agent's listing or evidence from a gardener at the property or a neighbour.

The second is through expert evidence. A knotweed expert will often be able to say that knotweed is more likely than not at least X years old. If this is before the sale of the property, the buyer can show that the property was affected.

The relevant time for when the property was affected is not the TA6 itself but the time of sale. This is clear from the wording of section 2(1) which provides for the time period "up to the time the contract was made" and is reinforced by the Law Society's explanatory notes which tell sellers that if they discover new information after completing the TA6 form, they must tell their solicitors of this.

Sometimes, buyers discover knotweed almost immediately after moving in. This is common if they purchase a property in early Spring and the seller had removed dead knotweed canes from the winter. As the growing season starts, knotweed might immediately grow in the garden and become obvious.

In other cases, the delay may be much longer. For instance, in an overgrown garden, buyers might only discover the knotweed growing amongst other undergrowth, perhaps behind a shed or other structure, one or two years after purchasing the property.

As one would imagine, the clearer the evidence is, the more straightforward it will be for the buyer to prove.

If knotweed is established as affecting the property at the time of sale then in a "No" case, the misrepresentation is made out. Under section 2(1), the next question is causation of loss which can be assumed for present purposes.

Under section 2(1) the burden then shifts to the seller to prove that:

i. They believed the representation to be true;

ii. They had reasonable grounds to believe it to be true.

The seller must prove that he believed his answer of "No" to be true. In some cases of obvious concealment (such as the seller cutting back the knotweed shortly before selling the property but leaving the remainder of the garden untouched) this may be difficult for the seller to prove. In other cases, it may be a minor issue because the buyer will be more concerned about the reasonable grounds argument.

The burden on the seller to establish reasonable grounds for his belief is a high one. The leading case on this point remains the Court of Appeal's decision in *Howard Marine & Dredging Co Ltd v Ogden & Sons (Excavations) Ltd* [1978] QB 574.

At 596 Lord Bridge described the effect of the Act in the following terms:

> *"In the course of negotiations leading to a contract the statute imposes an absolute obligation not to state facts which the representor cannot prove he had reasonable ground to believe."*

There is no authority on exactly what a seller must do to satisfy himself that he has reasonable grounds to believe there is no knotweed but my own view is that where a seller has done nothing, and ticks "No" simply because they do not think there is knotweed, that is unlikely to be enough.

If knotweed is established at the property at the time of sale in a "Not known" case, a claimant does need to show that the seller knew there was knotweed. If the seller did not know that there was knotweed, their answer of "Not known" was true and so there was no misrepresentation. The remainder of the claim would not get off the ground in those circumstances.

In my experience of "Not known" cases, the strong claims have been ones where there was a large growth of knotweed and the claimant is able to produce some evidence to show that the seller knew it was knotweed.

The knotweed must have been visible but even a large growth of knotweed alone may not be sufficient if the seller truly did not realise what it was.

Sometimes there may be evidence from a neighbour who will say that he discussed the problem of knotweed with the seller. There may be evidence from a gardener who worked for the seller and told them about the knotweed. There might be circumstantial evidence such as the seller concealing the knotweed.

If a misrepresentation is made out in a "Not known" case, that will generally be the end of the matter. Assuming causation of loss for present purposes, the seller cannot rely on a defence under section 2(1) if it has already been found by the court that they did know about knotweed at the property.

There is also the issue of questions 2.1 and 2.2 on the TA6 form relating to neighbour disputes. I also discuss these in Chapter Eleven. Some of the same evidence as in a "Not known" case under question 7.8 may apply – for instance if there is correspondence with a neighbour discussing the spread of knotweed.

CHAPTER THIRTEEN

RELIANCE

In any misrepresentation claim, the misrepresentation must have been relied on by the representee for there to be a claim.

The burden is on a claimant to prove that the misrepresentation was material, meaning that it was likely to induce them to enter into the contract. Given the prominence of the TA6 and the guidance notes, the questions therein are always likely to be treated as material.

Once the court finds that a misrepresentation was material, there is a presumption that the claimant was induced by it. It was said in *Hayward v Zurich Insurance Co Plc* [2016] UKSC 48 at para 37 that in a case of fraud, "it is very difficult to rebut the presumption". This will include a claim under section 2(1) of the Misrepresentation Act 1967 because of the fiction of fraud.

A claimant does not need to show that the misrepresentation was the sole inducement: it need only have been one of many.

Sometimes, a buyer will not obtain a homebuyer's report but instead will simply rely on the mortgage valuation report. Defendants will often say that they should not be liable for their answers on the TA6 form because the claimant should have had a survey and relied on that instead. There is no direct authority on this in a Japanese knotweed claim but the authorities tend to suggest that this is a weak argument.

In cases of rescission, it is no defence to say that the buyer might have discovered the falsity of the representation by taking reasonable care: *Redgrave v Hurd* (1881) 20 Ch D 1. That rule was paraphrased in *Laurence v Lexcourt Holdings Ltd* [1978] 1 WLR 1128 as follows:

> *"...it is well established that it is no defence to the person who has made the misrepresentation to say 'Oh well, the party who was misled could have checked and found out the facts for himself, and he really has only himself to blame that he relied on me and did not make the inquiries that he might have made.'"*

In a claim for damages under section 2(1) of the 1967 Act, the Court of Appeal accepted, albeit obiter, in *Taberna Europe CDO II Plc v Selskabet AF 1. September 2008 in Bankruptcy* [2016] EWCA Civ 1262, that a defence of contributory negligence may be available in principle.

The caveat to this is that it would likely be an exceptional case where the court did find that it would be just and equitable to make a finding of contributory negligence. The Court of Appeal referred to the judge's references at first instance to "the powerful statements of judicial opinion" in *Redgrave* and other cases. Those statements are summarised in the extract from *Laurence* above.

In the context of a Japanese knotweed claim, those statements are also consistent with the policy underlining the House of Lords' decision in *Smith v Eric S Bush & Harris v Wyre Forest District Council* [1989] 2 WLR 790 regarding a duty of care owed by surveyors to purchasers when carrying out a mortgage valuation survey. I discuss this in Chapter Sixteen.

It was held that a surveyor owes a duty to the purchaser despite the contract being between surveyor and mortgage lender because it is reasonably foreseeable that the purchaser will rely on the survey. This applies save for "very expensive houses".

Given this, the court is unlikely to find that a buyer was contributorily negligent for failing to obtain a homebuyer's report or specialist report on Japanese knotweed.

CHAPTER FOURTEEN

DAMAGES

The heads of loss in a misrepresentation claim are the same as in nuisance claims.

Generally, there may be damages for diminution in value, treatment costs and general damages for distress and inconvenience.

For diminution in value, the basic principles are the same in misrepresentation claims as in other claims. Just like diminution in nuisance claims in Chapter Six, the court is likely to award residual diminution in value plus treatment costs.

The key difference in misrepresentation claims is that it is the diminution is valued at the time of the sale of the property: *Smith New Court Securities Ltd v Citibank* [1997] AC 254.

If there are multiple defendants to a single claim, the surveyor will need to be asked to consider diminution at the time of sale for the misrepresentation claim and the current diminution for any other claims.

Those figures may be the same or may be different, usually depending on whether any work has been done to the property since it was purchased.

For treatment costs, the principles are the same as in nuisance claims.

As for distress and inconvenience, again this is likely to run in the same fashion as a nuisance claim. There is no authority on the level of damages but I have had misrepresentation claims where the parties have agreed that the court can take the same approach as the Recorder at trial in *Williams v Network Rail Infrastructure Ltd* [2019] QB 601, [2018]

EWCA Civ 1514. There, he awarded £350 per year though the knotweed infestation was serious.

CHAPTER FIFTEEN

RESCISSION

Rescission may be difficult where the seller has purchased another property and there is now a chain of transactions to untangle. There is no reason in principle, however, why a buyer cannot rescind a contract on the basis of a misrepresentation about Japanese knotweed.

The principles will be the same as in any other misrepresentation claim.

First, the buyer must not have affirmed the contract. There is no authority on this in a knotweed claim but an example of where the court may find that a buyer had affirmed would be a buyer who had building work done to the property after he had discovered it was affected by Japanese knotweed.

Secondly, there must not have been an undue lapse of time.

In both of these cases, the authorities are clear that there cannot be affirmation or a binding lapse of time until the representee discovered the misrepresentation. In the case of knotweed, there might be some delay before a buyer discovers that there is knotweed at the property and there was at the time of sale.

The court has a discretion to award damages in lieu of rescission under section 2(2) of the Misrepresentation Act 1967. This only applies where the requirements for rescission are met.

If the contract is rescinded, the court may order the seller to indemnify the buyer for obligations to third parties arising from the contract. There is no authority on this in a knotweed claim but this would be likely to include stamp duty charges, surveyor's fees and moving costs.

PART FOUR

PROFESSIONAL NEGLIGENCE CLAIMS AGAINST SURVEYORS

CHAPTER SIXTEEN

DUTY OF CARE

There are three types of pre-purchase survey: a mortgage valuation report, a homebuyer's report and a building survey.

A mortgage valuation report is done for the benefit of the mortgage lender but it is well-established that a surveyor who carries out such a report owes a duty of care to the purchaser because it is reasonably foreseeable that the purchaser will rely on it: *Smith v Eric S Bush & Harris v Wyre Forest District Council* [1989] 2 WLR 790 (HL).

In principle, a surveyor will therefore always owe a duty of care in negligence to a purchaser of a residential property. The exceptions may be commercial premises or what was described in *Smith & Harris* as "very expensive houses". There is no guidance in respect of this but given that the average house price in the UK at the time of writing is £285,000, I would suggest that it is difficult to see how anything less than four times this value could be described as "very expensive".

For homebuyer's reports and building surveys, the surveyor will also have a contract with the purchasers directly.

The duty of care will normally be the same in contract or negligence: to act to the standards expected of a reasonably competent surveyor. If there is no specific term pleaded in the contract, a promise to take reasonable care is implied by virtue of section 13 of the Supply of Goods and Services Act 1982.

I have never known it to be argued that a surveyor should not be expected to identify and report on Japanese knotweed if it is present.

Where the duty of care may differ in respect of the three different kinds of survey is the extent of the inspection required. For instance, a mortgage valuation report may not require a surveyor to look at neighbouring properties whereas for a homebuyer's report, readily visible knotweed on neighbouring land right up against the boundary with the subject property may be something which the surveyor is expected to identify and report.

CHAPTER SEVENTEEN

BREACH OF DUTY

The nature of establish breach against a surveyor will depend on the time of year of their inspection. The growing season for Japanese knotweed is normally from around March to October. Outside of the growing season, Japanese knotweed stems will die back and leave dead winter canes which remain unless removed.

Depending on the date of the survey, the question will be whether the surveyor should have identified live knotweed growth or dead winter canes.

The starting point for a claimant is to show that knotweed was visible at the date of inspection. It is not enough to say that there was knotweed at the property because this could have been concealed by the seller cutting it back or covering it. Alternatively, the knotweed might have been behind a shed or hidden in thick undergrowth where it was not there to be seen.

Knotweed may be visible in photographs taken by the surveyor on the day. Often there may be additional photographs taken by the surveyor which were not included in the report itself. A claimant will normally ask for these when sending a letter of claim.

There may also be photographs showing knotweed from the estate agent's listing which can normally be checked by searching online.

If Japanese knotweed is present in a prominent position in the garden but photographs show that it was not present on inspection, this may tend to suggest that the seller cut it back or concealed it. If the seller carried out a comprehensive makeover of the garden, this may not be surprising. If only the knotweed was removed, this may suggest that the seller deliberately concealed it.

This may make a claim weaker against a surveyor but stronger against a seller or vice versa.

If Japanese knotweed was present at the property but was obscured behind a shed or was located in undergrowth, it may be that a reasonable surveyor would not be expected to have identified it. Where there is a shed or some other obstacle, this will often turn on whether the knotweed was growing high enough to be visible above it. This will only apply to surveys carried out during the growing season.

As discussed in Chapter Sixteen, the type of survey may affect the scope of the inspection required. If there is Japanese knotweed growing in a neighbouring garden, right up against the boundary with the subject property, again the question will be whether this was visible. It may have been visible when looking out of an upstairs window or it may be that it was visible from the garden the fence. In some cases, there will be a palisade fence where knotweed can clearly be seen through the gaps rather than a solid fence.

All of these points will need evidence from an expert surveyor to comment on breach of duty.

CHAPTER EIGHTEEN

CAUSATION AND DAMAGES

A claimant must show that had the surveyor commented on Japanese knotweed, they would either have refused to purchase the property or would have only purchased it for a lower price.

Defendants may suspect such evidence to be self-serving but it is normally very difficult to challenge.

Where there is one or more concurrent claims in nuisance against a neighbouring landowner or against the seller for misrepresentation, each will generally be severally liable. I anticipate that they would not be jointly and severally liable because there is a different cause of action against each. The court might apportion damages between defendants itself or may award the claimant damages in full against each and leave it to the defendants to argue apportionment in a part 20 claim.

For damages in professional negligence, the starting point is the same as a nuisance claim, namely the residual diminution in value of the property plus treatment costs.

The timing of the diminution will be when the loss arises: *Philips v Ward* [1956] 1 WLR 471. In a knotweed case, this will normally be the time of sale.

An expert surveyor who is reporting on diminution in value will therefore need to be asked to comment on the diminution in value at the time of sale rather than the present diminution as in a nuisance claim. If there are concurrent claims both in nuisance and professional negligence, the surveyor will need to report on both.

For treatment costs, it does not matter when the knotweed encroached provided it was present and should have been reported on at the time of the survey.

A claimant may also be able to recover general damages for distress and inconvenience as in a nuisance claim. I discuss this in Chapter Eight.

As for the cost of any repairs, this would normally be a freestanding issue based on whether or not the surveyor negligently failed to report on the presence of any defects or damage to the property.

PART FIVE

PROFESSIONAL NEGLIGENCE CLAIMS AGAINST CONVEYANCERS

CHAPTER NINETEEN

CLAIMS AGAINST CONVEYANCERS

Most professional negligence claims will be against surveyors but there are cases where a claimant may consider a claim against a conveyancer.

The starting point is that a buyer's conveyancer will owe them a duty both in contract and in tort.

In contract, there may be an express term in the retainer or alternatively there will be the duty to act with reasonable care and skill implied into the contract by section 13 of the Supply of Goods and Services Act 1982.

In practical terms, the standard of care will not differ between contract and negligence.

In a standard purchase of a residential property, it would normally be expected of a conveyancer to ensure that the seller provided a completed copy of the Law Society's property information form ("the TA6 form"). If they did not, the buyer would not be able to rely on the various answers given within that form, including about Japanese knotweed at question 7.8.

If a conveyancer did not request this and it was not provided, the buyer may well have a claim. Likewise, a seller who did provide a form which answered "Yes" to question 7.8 but which was not then communicated to the buyer. In those circumstances, the buyer may well have a claim.

Sometimes, sellers will ask not to use the Law Society's standard conditions of sale, usually meaning also not using the TA6 form. This can be common with sales by local authorities, who often use their own standard terms of sale.

Depending on those terms, the seller may well not have to make any representation about Japanese knotweed at all. Alternatively, the terms may well exclude liability for any representations. A buyer may choose to accept these terms but the increased risks to the buyer would need to be explained in order for them to make an informed decision about this. If not, there may well be a breach of duty by their conveyancer.

In purchases of commercial properties, differing terms of this kind will often be common.

In terms of damages, these will generally be the same as in claims against surveyors.

PART SIX

PROCEDURE

CHAPTER TWENTY

LIMITATION

Nuisance claims are based on tort so the relevant limitation period is six years from the accrual of the cause of action under section 2 of the Limitation Act 1980 or 3 years from date of knowledge under section 14A of the Act. There is then a longstop date of 15 years under section 14B of the Act.

Where there has been encroachment, duty and breach for more than six years, claimants will rely on the principle of a continuing nuisance. That is to say, the clock continues to run so long as the defendant is in breach. If knotweed encroached in 2013 but a defendant only started to properly treat in 2018, the claimant would argue that the six years runs from 2018.

In *Jalla v Shell* [UKSC] 2023 16, it was held that a one-off oil spill was not a continuing nuisance. However, in para 30 it was said by Lord Burrows that:

> *"It can be seen that, on this analysis, a case on tree roots, such as Delaware Mansions, provides a good example of a continuing nuisance but need not be viewed as the paradigm example of a continuing nuisance. In such a case, there is an ongoing state of affairs outside the claimant's land, constituted by the living tree and its roots, for which the defendant is responsible and which causes, by extraction of water through its encroaching roots, continuing undue interference with the claimant's land. The cause of action for the tort of private nuisance therefore accrues afresh from day to day."*

In a knotweed case, there is an ongoing state of affairs on the defendant's land (untreated knotweed) which causes undue interference with the claimant's land. Therefore, the cause of action accrues afresh from day to day.

The defendant's counter-argument would be that once knotweed has encroached, the loss has been suffered. Both parties and the Supreme Court accepted in *Davies v Bridgend County Borough Council* [2024] UKSC 15 that this argument was not something which could or be resolved on the appeal. It will require expert evidence on the mechanics of the spread of Japanese knotweed and is bound to be the battleground for a future case.

The second argument is that under the principle of a continuing nuisance, a claimant can only recover the losses from within the last six years. That is common in tree root cases where particular cracking can be attributed to subsidence from different years. In a knotweed case, however, there is generally a single loss, namely the residual diminution in value after treatment. In those circumstances, a defendant may argue that this whole loss is out of time and should be disallowed.

I expect that the court would reject this argument given that when considering a single loss, to disallow that whole loss because it originated before the six-year limitation period would be to undermine the principle of a continuing nuisance and effectively to set a hard limit of six years. The compromise position of having the six-year limit but being able to ascertain which damages arose before and after, as in a tree root case, is simply not possible in a knotweed case.

What the court decides remains to be seen.

Date of knowledge may well be academic in many cases if the court accepts that the clock continues to run while a defendant remains in breach. Imagine a case where knotweed encroached in 2010, the defendant came under a duty to treat in 2012, the claimant discovered knotweed at their property emanating from the defendant's land in 2015 and the defendant started treating in 2017. In that case, the 3 year period from date of knowledge would expire in 2018 but the six year period from end of breach would expire in 2023. In that situation, the period from date of knowledge adds nothing. Date of knowledge may become more important if the court did find that that a claim for residual diminution in value and treatment costs was disallowable if it originated more than six years earlier.

As to knowledge, it is knowledge of "the material facts about the damage" per section 14A(six)(a) of the Act which in a knotweed claim will mean knowledge that Japanese knotweed is present at a claimant's property. It may arguably also mean that this will cause a diminution in value of the property. There is no authority about that.

Also, it is knowledge of the three factors in section 14(A)(8) of the Act, namely attributability, the identity of the defendant and if relevant, the identity of a third party. In this context, attributability is likely to mean knowledge that the knotweed has originated from the defendant's land.

In misrepresentation claims, the limitation period for a claim for damages under section 2(1) of the Misrepresentation Act 19six7 is six years under sections 2 and or/ 9 of Limitation Act 1980.

On the authority of *Green v Eadie* [2012] Ch 363, the limitation period runs from exchange of contracts rather than the misrepresentation or completion. In that case, it was held that the loss arose when the buyer became committed to the purchase. That occurred on exchange. At that point, the cause of action accrued: see para 57.

In a fraudulent misrepresentation claim or where there is deliberate concealment, a claimant may rely on section 32 of the Limitation Act 1980 which provides that the limitation period does not start to run until the claimant has discovered the fraud or concealment.

In professional negligence claims, a surveyor may have had a contract with the claimant. Certainly, in a claim against a conveyancer, there will be a contract. Where a surveyor conducted a mortgage valuation, they will owe a duty of care to a purchaser in negligence but there is no contractual relationship.

Therefore, depending on the circumstances, the relevant limitation period may be in contract, negligence or both. It is well-established that a duty in contract can run concurrently with a duty of care in negligence: *Henderson v Merrett Syndicates* [1995] 2 AC 145.

The primary limitation period for both is six years but for limitation will often be more favourable to claimants in negligence than in contract. For example, there is the 3-year period post-date of knowledge under section 14B of the Limitation Act 1980 for negligence claims.

It will normally be easier to identify when the cause of action accrued in a professional negligence claim because the negligence will relate to a specific act (e.g. the survey) rather than a continuing nuisance over a long period of time.

CHAPTER TWENTY-ONE

COSTS AND ALLOCATION

For many Japanese knotweed claims, damages will be comfortably above the £10,000 threshold for small claims. The usual costs rules will apply and depending on the value, the amount of evidence and the complexity of the issues, the case will either be allocated to the fast track, intermediate track or multi-track.

In cases where the value of the property is lower, damages may not reach the £10,000 threshold. If a claim is issued, the court may well allocate it to the small claims track in which case the very limited provision for costs would apply. In most knotweed cases, this will make it uneconomic for a claimant to fund the cost of litigation.

It may be that even in a low value claim, the amount and complexity of evidence would lead the court to allocate it to the fast track or intermediate track. Of course, from a claimant's perspective, they will not know this until directions stage, so they would have to take the risk in paying the issue fee and litigating the early stages of the claim before finding out.

What about a borderline case, where a claimant might seek damages of £15,000 but the court ultimately awards £8,000? The defendant will likely argue that the claimant unreasonably overvalued their claim and should be limited to small claims costs.

The court has a wide discretion on costs in these circumstances and so different judges will inevitably take different approaches. Many judges will say that if a claim has been allocated to a track where costs apply, the normal costs rules apply, even if the ultimate value awarded is below the small claims threshold.

My own view based on experience of claims in general is that if the claim can reasonably be valued at more than £10,000, the court will be likely to award costs even if the damages awarded are ultimately less. Only in a case where it was or should have been obvious that damages could not be above £10,000 will the court refuse to award normal costs.

Assuming a claim has not been allocated to the small claims track, in which case part 36 no longer applies, the parties can make part 36 offers which will provide for

reasonable costs in the normal way, even if the sums agreed are below £10,000. It may well be that a claim would be worth more than £10,000 if successful in trial but the claimant accepts a discount to account for litigation risk. That does not then put the case into the position of a small claim.

As to the question of fixed costs and complexity bands under the fast track and intermediate track, the position in knotweed claims is as uncertain as in all other civil claims. Over time, the dust will settle and parties will be able to predict with more certainty which complexity band of which track a particular court is likely to allocate.

PART SEVEN

OTHER INVASIVE SPECIES

CHAPTER TWENTY-TWO

OTHER INVASIVE SPECIES

Japanese knotweed is the most widely known invasive species of plant in the UK but there are many others.

As well as Japanese knotweed, formerly known as *Fallopica japonica* and now known as *Reynoutria japonica*, there is a similar species, *Reynoutria sachalinensis* aka "giant knotweed" which is also invasive.

There is also a variety of Japanese knotweed known as "dwarf Japanese knotweed" (*Reynoutria japnonica var. 'Compacta'*) which, as the name suggests, is smaller in size.

In the context of misrepresentation claims, the TA6 form refers to "Japanese knotweed". There is no authority on whether this extends to the dwarf variety and how the variety would affect the various questions in a claim under section 2(1) of the Misrepresentation Act 1967. There are arguments either way and no doubt this will be an important case in the future.

Apart from knotweed, a common invasive plant in the UK is giant hogweed *(Heracleum mantegazzianum)*. Unlike Japanese knotweed, giant hogweed is toxic to humans. This gives rise to new potential claims: for example, a landowner who fails to control a growth of giant hogweed which then injures walkers using a public footpath.

Himalayan balsam *(Impatiens glandulifera)* is another invasive plant. Unlike giant hogweed, it is not toxic.

Both are "controlled waste" within the meaning of the Environmental Protection Act 1990 and so must be disposed of in a designated fashion in the same way as Japanese knotweed.

This inevitably makes it more difficult for a landowner to develop their land which was part of the ratio in *Williams v Network Rail Infrastructure Ltd* [2019] QB 601, [2018] EWCA Civ 1514 as to why the presence of Japanese knotweed could amount to a nuisance.

As to diminution in value, neither would seem to be caught by question 7.8 of the TA6 form though if the seller knows of them and that they might spread, their presence might be caught by questions 2.1 and 2.2 of the TA6: see Chapter Eleven.

There is an argument as to whether a surveyor will be expected to identify them and report on them in a survey.

For farmers, another problematic species is black-grass *(Alopecurus myosuroides)*. This grass has developed herbicide-resistance and competes with crops for nutrients in the soil. The problem is well-known to farmers and one can see the building blocks for a nuisance claim.

Finally, bamboo has been the focus of a number of media articles recently. It has been known as an invasive plant for many years but again, the key difference between bamboo and knotweed is that bamboo is not asked about on the TA6 form. Therefore, the basis of a diminution in value (the disclosure of its presence and the consequent purchaser stigma) does not arise.

MORE BOOKS BY LAW BRIEF PUBLISHING

A selection of our other titles available now:-

'A Practical Guide to the Independent School Standards – September 2023 Edition' by Sarah McKimm
'A Practical Guide to Estate Administration and Crypto Assets' by Richard Marshall
'A Practical Guide to Managing GDPR Data Subject Access Requests – Second Edition' by Patrick O'Kane
'A Practical Guide to Parental Alienation in Private and Public Law Children Cases' by Sam King QC & Frankie Shama
'Contested Heritage – Removing Art from Land and Historic Buildings' by Richard Harwood QC, Catherine Dobson, David Sawtell
'The Limits of Separate Legal Personality: When Those Running a Company Can Be Held Personally Liable for Losses Caused to Third Parties Outside of the Company' by Dr Mike Wilkinson
'A Practical Guide to Transgender Law' by Robin Moira White & Nicola Newbegin
'A Practical Guide to 'Stranded Spouses' in Family Law' by Mani Singh Basi
'A Practical Guide to Residential Freehold Conveyancing' by Lorraine Richardson
'A Practical Guide to Pensions on Divorce for Lawyers' by Bryan Scant
'A Practical Guide to Challenging Sham Marriage Allegations in Immigration Law' by Priya Solanki
'A Practical Guide to Digital Communications Evidence in Criminal Law' by Sam Willis
'A Practical Guide to Legal Rights in Scotland' by Sarah-Jane Macdonald
'A Practical Guide to New Build Conveyancing' by Paul Sams & Rebecca East
'A Practical Guide to Defending Barristers in Disciplinary Cases' by Marc Beaumont
'A Practical Guide to Inherited Wealth on Divorce' by Hayley Trim
'A Practical Guide to Practice Direction 12J and Domestic Abuse in Private Law Children Proceedings' by Rebecca Cross & Malvika Jaganmohan

'A Practical Guide to Confiscation and Restraint' by Narita Bahra QC, John Carl Townsend, David Winch
'A Practical Guide to the Law of Forests in Scotland' by Philip Buchan
'A Practical Guide to Health and Medical Cases in Immigration Law' by Rebecca Chapman & Miranda Butler
'A Practical Guide to Bad Character Evidence for Criminal Practitioners by Aparna Rao
'A Practical Guide to Extradition Law post-Brexit' by Myles Grandison et al
'A Practical Guide to Hoarding and Mental Health for Housing Lawyers' by Rachel Coyle
'A Practical Guide to Psychiatric Claims in Personal Injury – 2nd Edition' by Liam Ryan
'Stephens on Contractual Indemnities' by Richard Stephens
'A Practical Guide to the EU Succession Regulation' by Richard Frimston
'A Practical Guide to Solicitor and Client Costs – 2nd Edition' by Robin Dunne
'Constructive Dismissal – Practice Pointers and Principles' by Benjimin Burgher
'A Practical Guide to Religion and Belief Discrimination Claims in the Workplace' by Kashif Ali
'A Practical Guide to the Law of Medical Treatment Decisions' by Ben Troke
'Fundamental Dishonesty and QOCS in Personal Injury Proceedings: Law and Practice' by Jake Rowley
'A Practical Guide to the Law in Relation to School Exclusions' by Charlotte Hadfield & Alice de Coverley
'A Practical Guide to Divorce for the Silver Separators' by Karin Walker
'The Right to be Forgotten – The Law and Practical Issues' by Melissa Stock
'A Practical Guide to Planning Law and Rights of Way in National Parks, the Broads and AONBs' by James Maurici QC, James Neill et al
'A Practical Guide to Election Law' by Tom Tabori
'A Practical Guide to the Law in Relation to Surrogacy' by Andrew Powell
'A Practical Guide to Claims Arising from Fatal Accidents – 2nd Edition' by James Patience
'A Practical Guide to the Ownership of Employee Inventions – From Entitlement to Compensation' by James Tumbridge & Ashley Roughton
'A Practical Guide to Asbestos Claims' by Jonathan Owen & Gareth McAloon

'A Practical Guide to Stamp Duty Land Tax in England and Northern Ireland' by Suzanne O'Hara
'A Practical Guide to the Law of Farming Partnerships' by Philip Whitcomb
'Covid-19, Homeworking and the Law – The Essential Guide to Employment and GDPR Issues' by Forbes Solicitors
'Covid-19 and Criminal Law – The Essential Guide' by Ramya Nagesh
'Covid-19 and Family Law in England and Wales – The Essential Guide' by Safda Mahmood
'A Practical Guide to the Law of Unlawful Eviction and Harassment – 2nd Edition' by Stephanie Lovegrove
'Covid-19, Brexit and the Law of Commercial Leases – The Essential Guide' by Mark Shelton
'A Practical Guide to Costs in Personal Injury Claims – 2nd Edition' by Matthew Hoe
'A Practical Guide to the General Data Protection Regulation (GDPR) – 2nd Edition' by Keith Markham
'Ellis on Credit Hire – Sixth Edition' by Aidan Ellis & Tim Kevan
'A Practical Guide to Working with Litigants in Person and McKenzie Friends in Family Cases' by Stuart Barlow
'Protecting Unregistered Brands: A Practical Guide to the Law of Passing Off' by Lorna Brazell
'A Practical Guide to Secondary Liability and Joint Enterprise Post-Jogee' by Joanne Cecil & James Mehigan
'A Practical Guide to the Pre-Action RTA Claims Protocol for Personal Injury Lawyers' by Antonia Ford
'A Practical Guide to Neighbour Disputes and the Law' by Alexander Walsh
'A Practical Guide to Forfeiture of Leases' by Mark Shelton
'A Practical Guide to Coercive Control for Legal Practitioners and Victims' by Rachel Horman
'A Practical Guide to the Law of Driverless Cars – Second Edition' by Alex Glassbrook, Emma Northey & Scarlett Milligan
'A Practical Guide to TOLATA Claims' by Greg Williams
'A Practical Guide to Elderly Law – 2nd Edition' by Justin Patten
'A Practical Guide to Responding to Housing Disrepair and Unfitness Claims' by Iain Wightwick

'A Practical Guide to the Law of Bullying and Harassment in the Workplace' by Philip Hyland
'How to Be a Freelance Solicitor: A Practical Guide to the SRA-Regulated Freelance Solicitor Model' by Paul Bennett
'A Practical Guide to Prison Injury Claims' by Malcolm Johnson
'A Practical Guide to the Small Claims Track – 2nd Edition' by Dominic Bright
'A Practical Guide to Advising Clients at the Police Station' by Colin Stephen McKeown-Beaumont
'A Practical Guide to Antisocial Behaviour Injunctions' by Iain Wightwick
'Practical Mediation: A Guide for Mediators, Advocates, Advisers, Lawyers, and Students in Civil, Commercial, Business, Property, Workplace, and Employment Cases' by Jonathan Dingle with John Sephton
'The Mini-Pupillage Workbook' by David Boyle
'A Practical Guide to Crofting Law' by Brian Inkster
'A Practical Guide to the Law of Domain Names and Cybersquatting' by Andrew Clemson
'A Practical Guide to the Law of Gender Pay Gap Reporting' by Harini Iyengar
'NHS Whistleblowing and the Law' by Joseph England
'Employment Law and the Gig Economy' by Nigel Mackay & Annie Powell
'A Practical Guide to Noise Induced Hearing Loss (NIHL) Claims' by Andrew Mckie, Ian Skeate, Gareth McAloon
'An Introduction to Beauty Negligence Claims – A Practical Guide for the Personal Injury Practitioner' by Greg Almond
'Intercompany Agreements for Transfer Pricing Compliance' by Paul Sutton
'Zen and the Art of Mediation' by Martin Plowman
'A Practical Guide to the SRA Principles, Individual and Law Firm Codes of Conduct 2019 – What Every Law Firm Needs to Know' by Paul Bennett
'A Practical Guide to Adoption for Family Lawyers' by Graham Pegg
'A Practical Guide to Industrial Disease Claims' by Andrew Mckie & Ian Skeate
'A Practical Guide to Conducting a Sheriff Court Proof' by Andrew Stevenson
'A Practical Guide to Vicarious Liability' by Mariel Irvine
'A Practical Guide to Applications for Landlord's Consent and Variation of Leases' by Mark Shelton
'A Practical Guide to Relief from Sanctions Post-Mitchell and Denton' by Peter Causton

Printed in Great Britain
by Amazon

61099752R00060